We're In This Together

We're In This Together

ENCOURAGEMENT FOR SEAFARERS

POINT COMFORT SEAFARERS' CENTER

Point Comfort Seafarers' Center
Point Comfort, Texas

Copyright © Point Comfort Seafarers' Center. All Rights Reserved.

ISBN: 978-1-954238-01-5

Contents

	Preface	1
1.	The Sea is Vast	3
2.	Tied Together	5
3.	Home Away from Home	7
4.	Relieving Monotony	9
5.	Shore Leave	11
6.	We Need Each Other	13
7.	Living Together	15
8.	Great Love	17
9.	The Light Shines	19
10.	In Control	21
11.	Caring for Each Other	23
12.	One Simple Thing	25
13.	Like the Village Fountain	28
14.	Welcome to Point Comfort!	31

Preface

Welcome to Point Comfort!
The book you hold in your hands is a symbol of our commitment to your support. The meditations and articles that we bring together here were written by members of our network who want to encourage you in your work and life of faith.

The Rev. Jim Abernathey is a retired priest of the Episcopal Church living in Palacios, Texas. He was ordained in 1970. Fr. Jim practiced civil engineering before entering the Episcopal Theological Seminary in Austin, Texas. He holds degrees from the University of Texas, the Episcopal Theological Seminary of the Southwest, and Rice University. He has served parishes in Palacios, Matagorda, Freeport, Silsbee, and Humble, all in Texas. He has six children, ten grandchildren, and four great-grandchildren.

The Most Rev. Brendan J. Cahill is Bishop of The Catholic Diocese of Victoria in Texas and, since 2017, the national Bishop Promoter of Stella Maris in the United States. He has been actively involved in port ministries for many years, first as a priest of the Archdiocese of Galveston-Houston. His leadership and experience in Stella Maris is a great benefit.

Susan Huppert is a writer for *The MARE Report* of the North American Maritime Ministry Association.

Photos throughout this book are from The Point Comfort Seafarers Center, unless otherwise noted.

CHAPTER 1

The Sea is Vast

By Rev. Jim Abernathey

Anyone who has ever gone through a severe storm at sea can relate to the ancient expression of awe and wonder: "O God, your sea is so vast and my boat is so small." Hatches are battened; lifelines are rigged; loose items are secured or tied down; the whole crew seems at the mercy of wind and wave, as indeed they are. We can only exercise good seamanship and pray for the storm to pass, confident that it will.

I am driven to the words of Psalm 107:23-32, and of how absolutely dependent we are on God's grace and mercy. We humans are only creatures, no matter how ingenious our inventions and plans, and all it takes is a storm (or an earthquake, or a mystery virus) to remind us of this. In the sacred season of Easter, when Christians celebrate the great and defining event of Jesus' resurrection, we are reminded that it is God who acts; all we can do is react.

Whatever your culture or background, O Mariner, remember that the end of your journey is to bring you closer to the one God, to whom the sailor cries in the storm. We are driven to trust God, because we discover we cannot trust our frail and fallible selves.

Fr. Jim Abernathey (Photo: Rhonda Cummins)

CHAPTER 2

Tied Together

By Rev. Jim Abernathey

So many things tie our planet together. If we simply examine the labels in our clothing, we find products from Bangladesh, Thailand, Costa Rica, Mexico, China, and Japan among others. Fellow humans in China, India, the Philippines, and South Africa (again, among others) consume rice and other grains from the United States and Canada. These are only some common examples. Steel, petroleum products, and others of the so-called "basic industries" are traded all over the world, and the vehicles tying it all together are the ships that sail the seas and the that seafarers who sail on them.

Anyone who spends much time around a major seaport encounters, in the seafarers, a wide range of nationalities from all over the world. We notice that any smooth-working crew is really a body of shipmates that must work together, and work cooperatively. From the captain to the deck hands and stewards, engine operators and quartermasters, the entire crew must work together if the ship and it functions are to be successful. I see an emerging parallel with the earth: this unique and lovely planet we all call home.

The earth is really a large spaceship. All of us, at any time, are living our lives as passengers. As with a ship and crew at sea, we need to work together to take care of the ship and each other. If we don't take care of our home, nobody else will.

Visiting seafarers receive a souvenir magnet to remember their visit to Point Comfort. (Photo: Captain of the MV Bow Chain)

CHAPTER 3

Home Away from Home

By Rev. Jim Abernathey

The life and work of a seafarer is not like life and work ashore. Obviously, the day to day location is different. While at sea or in a distant port, the working sailor is separated from home, family, kin, and friends of home. This familiar and beloved system of love and support may be thousands of miles away, with no prospects of return or contact for perhaps weeks or more.

As seafarers' center offers sailors an essential point of contact and support. Dependable electronic communication is an obvious example. An environment of friendly and caring support is available and ready. If there is some emergency back at home, the seafarer's center is a place where messages may be conveyed and ships agents may have direct and needed contact with crew members, and port Chaplains to offer pastoral support.

Although there is no substitute for home and family, the seafarers' center can offer some needed resources of a "home away from home" to the sailors. Any good seafarers' center exists to support and accommodate the sailors. There are communication opportunities, worship opportunities, and resources to assist crew members who may find themselves "strangers in a strange land". Seafarers' centers are important element in our godly gift of hospitality.

Ship visitor Rhonda Cummins helps welcome seafarers at Christmas 2019 (Photo: Tom Wise)

CHAPTER 4

Relieving Monotony

By Rev. Jim Abernathey

    I don't know how it is on merchant vessels, but aboard U.S. Navy warships it is not unusual to have some fun with brand-new shipmates. For example, a "handy billy" is a term for a small, portable pump. As a young midshipman aboard the destroyer escort USS Derby, I was once directed by a deck Chief to "go find Handy Billy and get him here on the double!" I scoured that ship from stern to stern, and every sailor I asked directed me to some obscure place, until one guy told me he had "seen Handy Billy ten feet aft of the fantail." I was halfway there when it dawned on me that "ten feet aft of the fantail" was in the water, and in the wake we were leaving behind!

    Do merchant sailors have some of the same kind of fun? Like sending someone on a quest for red and green oil for the port and starboard running lights? Seafarers the world over have their own humorous activities, all of which help relieve any monotony of days at sea in confined quarters.

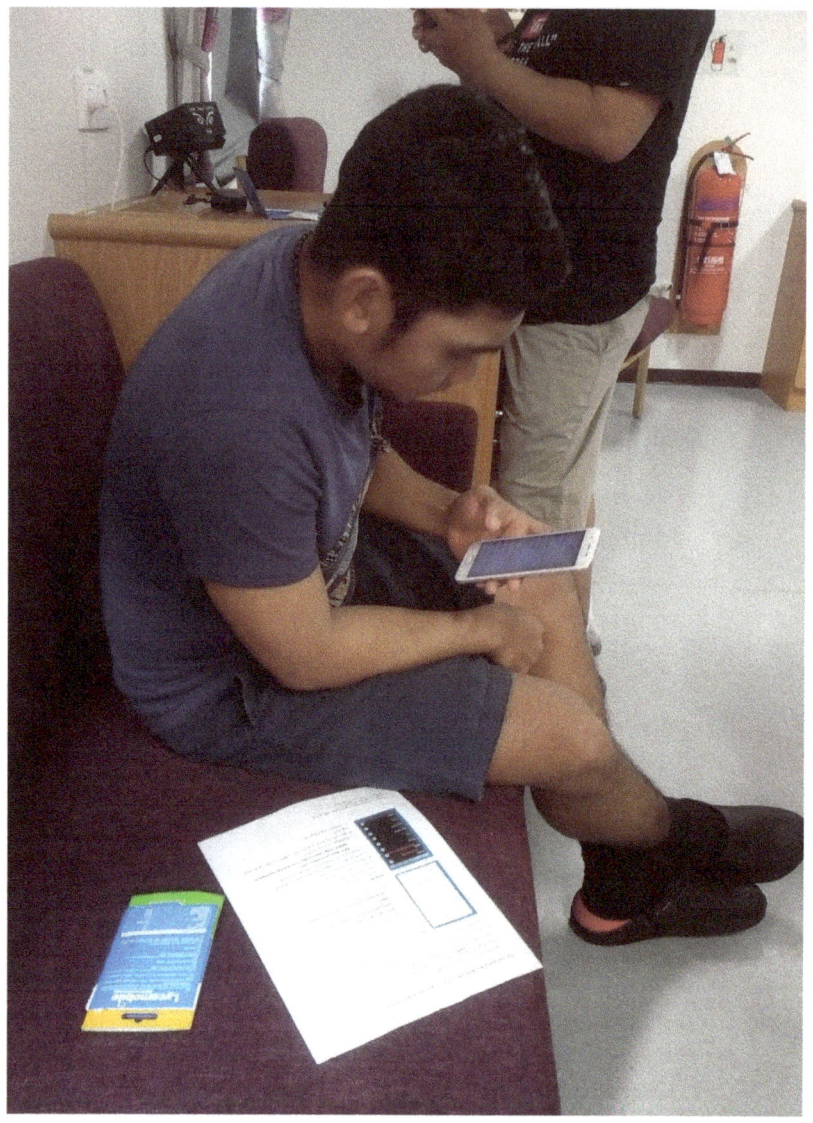

A seafarer loads a new SIM card into his phone so he can communicate with his family. (Photo: Rhonda Cummins)

CHAPTER 5

Shore Leave

By Rev. Jim Abernathey

Port liberty is a welcome time but also somewhat uncertain. Crew members are anxious to use dependable and available wi-fi, do some necessary shopping, and experience some of the recreational and cultural opportunities of a different part of the world. On the other hand, there are questions. How costly (and honest) is local transportation? Port commercial districts can attract all sorts of predatory opportunists, eager to relieve a seafarer of his or her money or possessions-what about these?

The local Seafarers' Center (if there is one) provides a safe and reasonable answer to these and other issues. At most centers, there are translation resources to assist the sailors, as well as access to good local transportation and local maps, along with safe and friendly recreational opportunities. The centers provide a ready and reliable place for communication with ship's agents and provide contact-points for medical or pastoral issues to be addressed. There are access and connections to religious and worship opportunities, as well as healthy connections to the local culture.

For the visiting seafarer, the center is a wonderful base of operations in a different country. The center is a place where he or she will not be exhibited or taken advantage of.

Seafarers are happy to have the chance to go shopping for essentials and some extra treats (Photo: Rhonda Cummins)

CHAPTER 6

We Need Each Other

By Rev. Jim Abernathey

In the face of the worldwide coronavirus pandemic, I sincerely hope that the seafarers of the world, along with the people they love, are managing to stay well and healthy. The men and women who sail the seas are isolated in two ways. First, they are part of a close-knit community aboard a ship at sea. They live together, work together, and eat together. In any port they visit (if they go ashore) they usually are together for shopping or recreation. This kind of community is separate from the life of the regular port residents.

Second, they have families and loved ones "back home", with who they seek to stay in touch. Problems at home are sources of worry and concern. Sailors are eager to have news of wives or husbands, children and grandchildren, other relatives and friends. If any are sick or in some other difficulty, this becomes an immediate matter of concern, worry, and prayer, along with the frustration of being apart and unable to help.

If a seafarers' center exists for the port, there are usually resources available to help a sailor communicate with his or her loved ones. Such available resources are among the most valuable things that can be made available to visiting seafarers. Local places of worship can provide pastoral assistance. We are all parts of a worldwide community. It is very important that everyone recognize this, whether we are at sea or ashore.

We need each other.

It is wonderful to see the smiles of seafarers who visit our port. (Photo: Rhonda Cummins)

CHAPTER 7

Living Together

By Rev. Jim Abernathey

In the United States Navy of a couple of generations ago, there were certain unwritten, but needy universal, rules for sailors ashore. The foundation rule pertained to one's ship and shipmates. No matter what controversies or arguments may be happening abroad, when ashore it was "all for one and one for all". Whether it was a sailor in a tight spot, a sailor in need, or a bar fight, you always rallied around your shipmate.

It's possible to break it down into a couple of general rules: (a) keep your area clean, and (b) don't let a shipmate down. You may dislike someone intensely on board-arguments may rage and even fights may occur-but ashore it's a different matter. Shipmates need to be able to count on each other when the chips are down. If, for some reason, they can't, then the whole ship will be in trouble. Keep your area clean and don't let a shipmate down.

That's not a bad set of rules for all of us. After all, this is our island home, and we need to care for our world and each other.

It is a joyful experience at Christmas to share presents with visiting seafarers. (Photo: Rhonda Cummins)

CHAPTER 8

Great Love

By Rev. Jim Abernathey

I have said it before and I believe it: Every well-run ship on the high seas is a kind of laboratory of a well-structured international society. Here at the port of Point Comfort, on the middle Texas coast, it is quite usual to find a vessel sailing under the Panamanian flag, but with an Italian captain, officers from a half-dozen different countries, and a crew consisting of Filipinos, Middle Easterners, West Africans, and North Americans. Within this onboard community are Muslims, Buddhists, Roman Catholics, Eastern Catholics, European Protestant Christians, and those professing no religious faith at all.

As A Christian priest, I insist that each one is a beloved child of a divine Creator, a God who blesses the whole of creation with life-giving rain and sunshine, and who inspires us all with the breath of life. All of it is a great act of love. Such love is demonstrated in mutual respect, in the harmony of working together for the common well-being, in the commitment to do what is necessary to help each member of the ship's company have a successful voyage and to sail the ship safely and well.

Every job or rating on board is important and every person onboard is important. None of this means that disagreements won't occur or that fights won't break out. They can and they do. But underlying everything is the fact that we are all onboard together, and that each shipmate is a brother or sister. For me, that is the lesson of the successful seagoing community. I wish the world would learn it politically.

Though modern technology is helpful to avoid problems, seafarers still need to look out the windows for dangers. (Photo: Rhonda Cummins)

CHAPTER 9

The Light Shines

By Rev. Jim Abernathey

In the Christian Scripture, we read in the Gospel according to St. John (1:5) "The light shines in the darkness, and the darkness did not overcome it."

Regardless of your spiritual background or awareness, this is an eternal and self-evident truth. And even a small or partial, light always prevails over darkness.

Some years ago, I had a beloved dog – a small Australian terrier named Murphy. He slept on a pillow next to my bed and, as we both grew older, each of us would have to make at least one "relief trip" during the night. Murphy and I were synchronized enough so that our trips usually coincided. Ever the gentleman, Murphy never barked. He would meekly come to me beside the bed and sort of clear his throat. I would get up and the two of us would begin our trip to the back door to let Murphy out.

I had a very small light near my bathroom door (for my benefit), but as we went through the house and moved away from that tiny light, it was always apparent to me that we were moving into the darkness-a darkness that seemed to grow around us and threaten to swallow us up. After letting Murphy out and turning back toward my bedroom and bathroom, I was always aware of the transforming influence of that little light. As I moved toward the light, however small, the way was visible and clear.

For me, it was a parable. I believe it is an eternal parable. Seek the light; always move toward the light, and you will find the true way. Shine the light of honesty to expose and overcome corruption and falsehood. Shine the light of truth to expose and overcome lies. Shine the light of kindness-shine the light of mercy-shine the light love-shine the light of peace -and cruelty, greed, hatred, and selfishness will be exposed for what they are.

"The light shines in the darkness, and the darkness did not overcome it."

We love to serve seafarers in action, but also enjoy a friendly conversation. (Photo: Tom Wise)

CHAPTER 10

In Control

By Rev. Jim Abernathey

   Once aboard the USS Darby (a World War II-era destroyer escort), I experienced a 48-degree roll. It was quite a thing. You could hear things happening all over the ship: furniture breaking loose, some deck gear shifting, loose items being tossed around, and a host of smaller noises. Upon the signal bridge, there were reports of sailors grabbing frantically for any handhold as normal lines of sight revealed only a boiling and angry sea. After the storm had passed, inspections showed some broken instruments and damaged steam lines, as well as areas requiring serious cleanup.

   Modern vessels are superbly designed examples of naval architecture and technology, but any sailor knows that once at sea, the real boss is wind and wave, tide and current. The forces and influences that have been around since creation still prevail and are always present. At sea, humans are always reminded that they are not, ultimately, in control. It is God's world, and not ours. Whatever your religion or spiritual persuasion, it is a power greater than ourselves that ultimately prevails. In the face of this, a kind of unwritten law of the sea is that any vessel in the vicinity responds to a ship and crew in distress. You don't pass up fellow seafarers in peril.

   These unwritten rules are not always observed, it's sad to say. Politics get in the way. But the oceans neither know nor care about such man-made things. They pass, and God, whose love and care are the same for every nook and cranny of the created order, desires only that all creatures live in peace and harmony with God and each other.

It is a special treat to enjoy a pleasant conversation with a visiting crew. (Photo: Rhonda Cummins)

CHAPTER 11

Caring for Each Other

By Rev. Jim Abernathey

One of the greatest joys of being a local pastor is the opportunity to be allowed into the inner and personal lives of the people entrusted to your care. I have been an Anglican priest for 50 years, and am blessed to have dear friends and shared memories from the very beginning.

I'm sure that the same is true for anyone, ordained and set apart for pastoral ministry. Although we may hear or read reports of betrayals by some who have been granted this trust, I am convinced that these are the rare exceptions and not the rule. I took vows at my ordination, before God and witnesses, and those vows are at the core of my being, and I am sure the same is true for every pastor of every tradition.

For seafarers, who spend long periods away from home sailing the oceans of the world, it is very important that there be shoreside opportunities for pastoral care and contact. Even modest facilities, like those of our team in Point Comfort, Texas, can fill this role. Our ship visiting team can do some important shopping, and the churches and agencies of our location on the middle Texas coast contribute to our courtesy and welcome parcels for the officers and crew of each visiting ship. These are small but genuine ways in which we say "welcome" and "howdy" to the sailors who come our way. One of our hopes and prayers is to open doors that will help us obtain a more inviting and permanent facility, with even more services.

Such contact also forges relationships at the most important level: the human one. The God who has brought us all, and everything else, into being embraces all that is. There are no nationalities with God, and there no nations. God has made of one blood all the peoples on earth and has brought us all into being in a giant act of love.

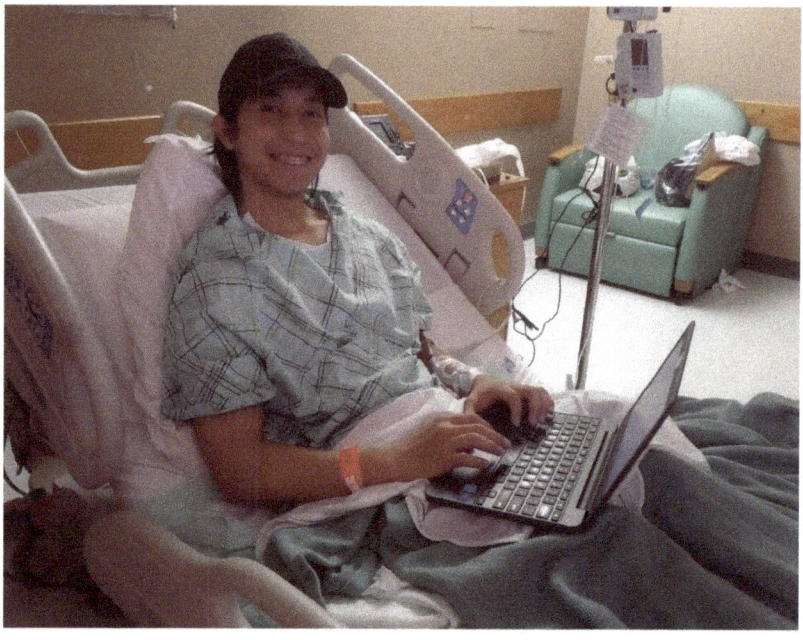

Sometimes seafarers need medical care ashore. Our seafarers' ministry visits them when they are in hospital. (Photo: Rhonda Cummins)

CHAPTER 12

One Simple Thing

by Bishop Brendan Cahill, Diocese of Victoria, Texas

 On Pentecost Sunday 2020, Bishop Shelton Fabre of Houma-Thibodeaux delivered a homily reflecting on the reality of racism in light of the death of George Floyd. One of the questions he addressed for the listeners was: "what can I do?" In speaking to those who were not African-American he invited us to do one simple thing. That simple thing was to ask an African-American friend: "how did seeing the video of George Floyd's death make you feel?" In asking the question he asked us to give space for the person to respond. I remember hearing clearly in the response of one friend an expression of deep pain.

 The feelings brought up by that event and the following weeks have run deep. I know that many of our chaplains and seafarers have had powerful conversations about race and justice in the light of the Gospel message of Jesus Christ. These conversations can be extremely intense and often we may desire to avoid them for another day. When we do have the courage to share and listen, with openness to one another's feelings and thoughts, a pathway to hope and a better day become possible. The pathway is one marked out by our ministry – striving to be a listening heart for another.

 The ministry of the listening heart is evident in so many stories I hear from chaplains around the country and the world. On May 22, 2020 we were able to offer our prayer for mariners on a video conference call from locations like Jacksonville, Florida; Seattle, Washington; Washington, DC; Charleston, South Carolina; Port Arthur and Point Comfort, Texas and others. In listening to the prayers from around the country I heard men and women who are present to brothers and sisters in challenging times related to the pandemic. Seafarers know they are not alone and there is someone who will stand up and join a voice with theirs. May our voices continue to bring to others the blessings and the challenges of the seafarers' vocation.

I want to conclude here with inspiring words that come from the first encyclical letter written by Pope Francis over six years ago. Calling us to be a Church not afraid to have difficult conversations he wrote in *Evangelii Gaudium*:

"49. Let us go forth, then, let us go forth to offer everyone the life of Jesus Christ. Here I repeat for the entire Church what I have often said to the priests and laity of Buenos Aires: I prefer a Church which is bruised, hurting and dirty because it has been out on the streets, rather than a Church which is unhealthy from being confined and from clinging to its own security. I do not want a Church concerned with being at the center and which then ends by being caught up in a web of obsessions and procedures. If something should rightly disturb us and trouble our consciences, it is the fact that so many of our brothers and sisters are living without the strength, light and consolation born of friendship with Jesus Christ, without a community of faith to support them, without meaning and a goal in life. More than by fear of going astray, my hope is that we will be moved by the fear of remaining shut up within structures which give us a false sense of security, within rules which make us harsh judges, within habits which make us feel safe, while at our door people are starving and Jesus does not tire of saying to us: "Give them something to eat" (Mk 6:37)."

May God bless you and your families throughout this summer season, and may you continue to have the strength to offer the true food of love and compassion. Let's entrust our hearts to the Sacred Heart of Jesus and the Immaculate Heart of Mary and let's keep one another in prayer,

+Brendan

Bishop Brendan Cahill and Sr. Rosario Resendez, IWBS preparing Christmas gifts for seafarers (Photo: Rhonda Cummins)

CHAPTER 13

Like the Village Fountain

by Bishop Brendan Cahill, Diocese of Victoria, Texas

A few years ago someone was preaching about St. John XXIII and the person quoted some words of the saintly Pope. St. John XXIII hoped for the Church to have a motherly face. He believed that her task was to keep "her arms open to receive everyone," and be a "home for one and all" that "desires to belong to everyone, and in particular she is the Church of the poor, like the village fountain."

As we are preparing to celebrate the birth of our Lord and Savior, it remains striking to see that he wasn't born in a palace or castle. Mary gave birth to a Son in a manger, with the just and humble Joseph protecting her and her Child. The beauty of the art and music that portray this event and the childhood of Jesus shine brightly the mission of the Church. We have come to believe that this Child brings hope and healing to the world, and we go out with energy to proclaim the beauty and potential for every child. Like the village fountain, we give water to everyone, with no distinction.

How blessed we are to proclaim this Good News through the work of Stella Maris and all seafarers' ministries! All of our work and actions are powerful in themselves and are made even more powerful when connected to the love of God and humanity shining forth from that manger in Bethlehem 2000 years ago.

St. John XXIII prayed a simple prayer every day that kept him connected with Jesus. It was a commitment of 10 things each day and is called the daily Decalogue of Pope John XXIII. I think this could be a powerful prayer for us as we celebrate the Christmas season and begin to make our commitments for another year:

1. Only for today, I will seek to live the livelong day positively without wishing to solve the problems of my life all at once.

2. Only for today, I will take the greatest care of my appearance: I will dress modestly; I will not raise my voice; I will be courteous in my behavior; I will not criticize anyone; I will not claim to improve or to discipline anyone except myself.

3. Only for today, I will be happy in the certainty that I was created to be happy, not only in the other world but also in this one.

4. Only for today, I will adapt to circumstances, without requiring all circumstances to be adapted to my own wishes.

5. Only for today, I will devote 10 minutes of my time to some good reading, remembering that just as food is necessary to the life of the body, so good reading is necessary to the life of the soul.

6. Only for today, I will do one good deed and not tell anyone about it.

7. Only for today, I will do at least one thing I do not like doing; and if my feelings are hurt, I will make sure that no one notices.

8. Only for today, I will make a plan for myself: I may not follow it to the letter, but I will make it. And I will be on guard against two evils: hastiness and indecision.

9. Only for today, I will firmly believe, despite appearances, that the good Providence of God cares for me like no one else who exists in this world.

10. Only for today, I will have no fears. In particular, I will not be afraid to enjoy what is beautiful and to believe in good-

ness. Indeed, for 12 hours I can certainly do what might cause me consternation were I to believe I had to do it all my life.

May God bless you and your families with peace and good health this Christmas season and may we be like the village fountain that gives water to all who are thirsty!

+Brendan

An amazing puzzle finished and signed. A small gift from us became a memorable activity on this ship. (Photo: Rhonda Cummins)

CHAPTER 14

Welcome to Point Comfort!

by Susan Huppert, NAMMA

Smaller ports are significant when the measure is not volume of cargo or the speed of exchange, but care for seafarers. Seafarers' welfare work in the Port of Point Comfort, Texas, with only five deepwater berths and 6 barge slips, deserves attention for its personalized care.

Ship visitor, Rhonda Cummins, an Episcopalian, calls on seafarers in Point Comfort. Working jointly with Stella Maris, the Catholic maritime charity, she views the port as "tiny" compared to others like Corpus Christi or Houston. Yet, regarding the impact on seafarer's lives it is far from tiny.

When ships dock, international seafarers commonly search for people who have their interest at heart. Seafarer ministries and ship visitors fill that role. Those living and working at sea feel a sense of trust when they hear a ship visitor is from the "Stella Maris" or the "Seamen's Mission." They need someone they can trust and Cummins and her team are those people at Point Comfort.

Christmas presents ready to distribute to seafarers in December 2020. (Photo by Janet Jones, Diocese of Victoria)

"She is just on fire," said the Most Reverend Brendan J. Cahill, Bishop of the Diocese of Victoria, Texas, and serves as the Apostleship of the Sea, Bishop Promoter for the United States. Bishop Cahill encourages seafarers' welfare in ports around the country, but is especially happy to support the work of Rhonda Cummins and her team in his own diocese.

"Seafarers need a friend in every port," said Cummins, Volunteering her time in conjunction with the Catholic mission. "I am trying to fill that void."

"She is a woman filled with faith, commitment and zeal," said Cahill, who Cummins views as a key partner along her way.

"She is a person who is passionate about this ministry."

Cahill believes she has a story to tell and a call to fulfill. He helps by encouraging, listening and giving her time. As financial needs arise, Stella Maris assists.

Cummins' goal is to create something at Point Comfort that will be as self-sustaining as possible and flexible enough to grow with the changes in the port and industry. This will take time and patience. She contends that a carefully thought out and tailored solution should be able to stand the test of time.

The Reverend Tommy Chen, priest of Our Lady of the Gulf

Catholic Church is a port chaplain for Point Comfort's budding outreach. He celebrates Mass with seafarers when requested and able. Chen also supplies Bibles in the Tagalog language and his parish donates generously when asked for donations for care packages or Christmas gifts.

Point Comfort is part of the Calhoun Port Authority, a key gateway to world markets for the Texas mid-coast region. The port plays a vital role in supporting Texas chemical manufacturing industries and in building a stable economic foundation for Calhoun County.

Woven within this economic exchange is the nascent seafarers' mission, extending itself without a physical center or team of paid staff. As the mission grows these services will come. Yet, because they are still small, they can give personalized care to visiting seafarers.

As bishop promoter of port missions within the Catholic Church nationwide, Cahill feels Point Comfort is likely to grow and this ministry along with it. He is confident the church will get behind it even more.

"Right now, all you have is people who care," said Cummins. "I am living out my faith tradition which is to welcome the stranger. I walk along the port, smile, wave and remind seafarers that they are not forgotten."

"She is a beautiful example of someone's journey to serve," said Cahill.

During the 2019 Christmas season Cummins coordinated donations from more than 40 organizations including Cub Scouts, churches, families and individuals to fill and deliver 517 Christmas boxes to seafarers on 31 vessels at Point Comfort. Christmas 2020 saw the collection and delivery of 709 gifts.

Although COVID-19 curtails contact with seafarers to a great degree, Cummins finds the opportunities to deliver more than requested. Recently, an opportunity when a ship's agent messaged the Point Comfort Facebook page that a ship captain had a special request for "cleaning wipes". Cummins made a care package for the ship including the request and much more, leading to multiple gangway visits since to deliver care packages and magazines to the crews unable to leave the ships.

She is looking for opportunities not limitations. In the coming years the ministry will continue to grow, strengthening the volunteer base, making the right partnerships, and considering new services that could help seafarers. If a location within walking distance of the ships can be arranged, Cummins suggests an ecumenical center with internet access to serve seafarers around the clock.

Cummins has her ear to the ground for such provisions and her eyes toward the ships so that many seafarers can hear "Welcome to Point Comfort!"

Welcome to Point Comfort!

www.ingramcontent.com/pod-product-compliance
Lightning Source LLC
Chambersburg PA
CBHW040311050426
42449CB00019B/3485